Death

When The Time Comes...

"...Then, with joy exploding
Into God's universe we go,
without foreboding.."

Death

Poems For The Grieving Heart
by D.N. Sutton

Copyright © 1994 & 2000 by D.N. Sutton
All Rights Reserved
Cover By Ida Candelaria

ISBN: 0-940361-21-3
Printed in USA by Acorn Press

Sherwood-Spencer Publishing
The SoulSite Press: www.SoulSite.com
The SoulSite Shop: soulsite.com/shop
The SoulSite Library: soulsite.com/library
SoulSite Contact: sutton@soulsite.com

For My Father
The "Brave Rider" whose joyous life experience
and swift death inspired many of these poems.

Death

Poems For The Grieving Heart

Brave Rider	1
Death Is Not Doom	2
New Hills	3
Clear Bell	4
Proud Galleon	5
Heroes' Shore	6
My Mother Sleeps	7
I Will Not Weep	8
Grief Grown Small	9
Sweet Goddess	10
Death Song	11
Even Though I Go	12
Elegy For A Young Traveler	13
Teenage Touchdown	14
Empty Spaces	15
I Will Go Into Death	16
Incline	17
High Wire	18
When I Lie Dying	19
And So One Day	20
Death Duel	21
For Sylvia Plath	22
Karen, Are You Myth?	23
When The Heart Is Eager	24
Small Death, Large Life	25
You Will Not Leave Unknown	26
Person Unparalleled	27
Too Soon For Tumbleweed	28
Know Only Joy	29
Is It Ever Too Late?	30

Brave Rider

Sing out
O dying heart
To the new unknown-ness.
Throw your life's lariat
And mounting the swift horse of change
Ride beautifully into the beyond!

In earth's energies
Harnessing for entry
Into the raceways of the Infinite
Deny terror.
Gladly go, with
Sweet, bruised banners flying
Saddled in the tender Allness of the Father.

You, O hero-child
Coming at the call
Let go the shadowed body
Consciousness trailing dreams like smoke
And loosening all reins
Ride out
Cutting a bright new swath
In the terrain of the eternal.

Sing out
Brave rider
And with God's own breath
Put the lie
To man's small dream of death.

Death Is Not Doom

Death is not doom
Take the loved one's leaving
Without grieving
With joy
Knowing
Death is transition
The return trip home.

We, on loan to life, on holiday
Come from God's place
Go back again
Adventure done
New phase begun.

Death is the ultimate move
Homecoming
Warm welcome
Healing.
Dark symbols, grim thoughts
Are error
Eliminate terror
Joy is the feeling.

Death is drama
End is beginning.
Trauma
Lies in forgetting
The larger plan
We are not God
But human.

New Hills

Now you are going
As you came
Alone
Slipping down the misted path
Footsteps fading
Crumbling stones quiet.

Still in our mind's eye we see you
Your climb up the hillside
Brave, headstrong, dashing
And now your descending again
Into the uncharted canyons of your being
Eyes conveying bewilderment, hurt
Body thrashing refusal.
Still, faithful to your longings
You linger only to leave
Wanting to go
Knowing you are gone.

We listen
Catch in throat
Until
Sensing your leap over the barriers
We hear your whoop of joy
At finding new hills ahead.

Clear Bell

So now you are in transit
Magnificent barge of life cut loose
Drifting downstream to the open sea
Of death.

You go, a king
Nobility clear
Liability softened
Love, the one strand left
Linking you to us on shore
Ego gone, body crumbling
Love lights the passage fore and aft
Sounding a clear bell from soul to soul.

Go now in majesty...
Calm currents bear you
Out of narrow waters
To oceanic space
Compass pointing
To your star.

Proud Galleon

I saw you go with my own eyes
The proud galleon of your life
Set sail
Leaving harbor mouth for ocean swells
Old landmarks
For unfamiliar seas.

You left, log clear
Course set
Past the rocky point
Trailing a clean wake
Into deeper waters
Tide impelling you
Beyond sight
But not beyond love.

Bonds
Stronger than vows
Surge with you
As swift currents
Bear your noble craft
To its destined harbor.

Heroes' Shore

King, Viking
Inspired passage to you
In your wondrous craft of Death.

Winds sanctified to bear you
Sweep you beyond the headlands
To seas vaster than your visions.

Strong flashes of memory
Of your selfless courage
Freedom from all guile
Illuminate the night-sky of our grief
As compass unknown,
Your valiant vessel courses
To the heroes' shore.

My Mother Sleeps

My mother sleeps in the cave of the winds
Water lapping on silver stones
Does not disturb her ancient bones.
Sometimes she stirs; her lidded eyes
Open and close: she smiles, sees
Then sleep transcends.

My mother lies on a golden litter
Life suspends
Her bed, her bier
Sensing always that love is near.

My mother hears the silken sounds
Of planets whirring
Music playing
A child again she feels the warmth
Of sunlight streaming
Past, present fuse in her dreaming
No shadow falls on her unseen walls.

My mother lives on
In unknown space
Lingering in a state of grace.
My mother awaits
Her final leaving
Her life, her death
Interweaving.

I Will Not Weep

I will not weep for Frances
I will not weep
I will think of her asleep.

I will forget
Her pain
My own
I will let
Grief alone.

I will accept
Fate fullfilled
Beauty distilled.

I will think of her awake
Life unfinished
Legacy of love
Undiminished.

Grief Grown Small

Frances
You are gone
Filling other spaces
With the fragrance of yourself
But still here with us
In these places
Cameo gift
Softening death's rift.

Instinctive southern belle
Exquisite beauty
Your essence everywhere
In the garden, on the stair.

You made spacious
Narrow corridors
With gracious talk
Voice birdsong
In the parlored air.
Spirited, yet soft, serene
Unconscious echo
Of the ante-bellum scene.

Mystique lingers on
Grief grown small
More penetrable now
The magnolia wall.

Sweet Goddess

Goddess
Sweet Goddess
Remembered...

You still stand
In mind
In heart
Classic work of art
Grecian statue
But intact
Nothing missing
Not fingers
Hands or toes
Nor chip off the chiselled nose
No dent in the flawless chin
Your damage did not show
It was within.

Internally, unseen
Cancer took you from us
Piece by piece
Ravaging the inner courtyards
Of your being
Tearing down the barricades
Of your splendid self.

In your coffin you lie radiant
As though fresh from an historic grave
An archaeological find
Discovered in an ancient Eastern field
Now poised to ascend into the present life
Adorn our personal museums
Ilumine our darkened lives
Painting over our pain
With the poetry
Of your desperately needed beauty.

Sweet Goddess
You still stand
In our souls
You stand.

Death Song

Do not be sad
My husband
Do not be sad
Rejoice with me
My darling
Make your spirit glad.

Do not weep
My husband
Do not weep
Think of me
As always
Smiling in my sleep.

Do not grieve
My husband
Do not grieve
There are sweet mysteries
Beyond this life
If only we believe.

Love so vast
My dearest
Love so vast
Was never meant to perish
But to last.

So do not fear
My darling
Do not fear
Hold me close forever
Keep love's presence near.

Even Though I Go

Even though I go
I will never leave you
I will love you from behind the veil
Through the mist
Be with you, hold you.

Memory brings
A cooling touch
A warming hand
A playful message in the sand.

Even though I go
Still I stay
In the silken air
The emerald pool
I will not be far away.

If you call me
I will come
Bring butterflies
Spark the brightness
In your eyes.

Elegy For A Young Traveler

Now his pillow is a star
Now he lays his head upon it
Even though he is afar
God's love is with him every minute.

Now the nightwind cools his brow
Now the sunlight warms his limbs
Now the planets dance and bow
And sing out joyful hymns.

The young prince moves across the skies
Angels bear him as he lies
There are snowflakes in his crown
Clouds are ermine in his gown.

Propelled by earthling's rain-soft tears
He sails among the heaven's spheres
He has God's promises to keep
And, smiling, keeps them while we weep.

Teenage Touchdown

He is taking off to find you
Knows you are there
Sky Mother, Grandmother
He seeks you
Longs for you,
Uncomprehending.

He does not quite grasp
He has made it over the great divide.
Circling in over the rim
He is descending
Eyes open wide, vision dim
Still loosely hanging on to the controls.

Some, like comets, enter flaming
But he is wafting, sometimes aware
As brilliance gleams, then fades.

He senses, loved Grandmother,
You are in the tower
Awaiting his touchdown
His finest hour now
A circling spiral to your open arms.

Empty Spaces

So still the beach
Lonely bay
Grasses listless in the wind
Since you went away.

You filled it all
No one knew
Until the empty spaces
Wept for you.

I Will Go Into Death

I will go into death
Singing
If I have breath.

And there is no doubt
I will be dancing
In life I could not do without
So I will dance
In death.

One thing I know
I will be laughing
At the wry joke
Of singing
Even as I choke.

And dancing
Even as I lie,
Such an unconventional notion
Of a way to die.

Incline

In the body's long dip
Into the decline of death
There is incline
Upsurge of soul, spirit
Awareness of the world
And all that's in it
New perception
Bringing resurrection.

It is nature's enduring charity
A given
Sent by heaven
That obscurity be
Replaced with clarity.

High Wire

In the matchless dance of life
There is discernment of death
A quieting
Where once
A lively stepping
A calming
Of intense pursuit.

The high wire of our being
Held taut at either end
Slackens
Even as it quivers
With the music of our souls.

The dance goes on
Tempo alters
But not the melody
Life and death entwine
In destined harmony.

When I Lie Dying

When I lie dying
Kiss my lids
My lips
My hair
So I sense you there.

Hold me
In that flame and light
That clean eclipse
Before my astral flight
Stars, bright pebbles
On a lofty beach
Within our reach.

And So One Day

And so one day
You will ripple down on me
From a high space
Winging in
And I
Running on the beach
Will see you coming
Silver winged
Sparkling tipped
Singling me out.

I will feel my heart extend
In its furthest reaching
I to you
You to me
You will embrace me in your velvet wing-span
And I will lighten
To be lifted
Leaving behind my song
And an empty, unneeded shell.

Death Duel

Oh, my child
I sensed death
As death drew near
Wings beat
Close to my ear
Deep fear.

I felt heat
In the night's cold
Short breath
Blue vein
Sharp cry
Profound pain.

I sensed death
Death came,
Death hovering
At the year's end
I shivered at
Its grim portend.

But I held death off
With scorn and shame
Vows, fury, passion, blame
I held it at bay
As judge and jury
Blew all logic
With threats and pleading
Sank to wheedling
Playing the game
Of praise and blunder
Panic and of prayerful wonder.

I raised heaven and earth
Bruised the conscience
Of saint and devil
Imploring end of this struggle
Anything to save my child.

Storm done
Wildness settled
Dawn came in
And I, embattled
Saw you live,
Death gone.
Oh, my child!

For The Poet, Sylvia Plath
1932 - 1963

Even after long years
Death by one's own hand
Still evokes pain...
Bewilderment and sadness
In those who remain.

What if you were deliberately to die
Would you do it silently
Without outcry
Put your head
In an oven, vomit gas
While babies cry?

Or if you could, would you
Seek a more poetic setting
Just as swift
Without bloodletting
Perhaps on the beach
Where giant breakers welling
Spew salt tears
Broken dreams expelling?

If choice were yours
Would you go in sorrow
Or in soaring
With all the love
Of life and God
Outsinging
And outpouring?

The truth is
Who would choose to go at all
Unless that compelling call
Hurled one through
The barrier wall?

Sylvia
We grieve for you...

Karen, Are You Myth?

Where are you, Karen?
Where, when the sun's gold fingers
Warm the world, are you?
Where, when the night turns velvet
Do you lie, no arms to hold you
Dreaming dreams dead as fallen leaves?

Do you still live, are you still here?
You, your hair shining, your walk music
No one's thought more crystalline than yours,
Are you memory, now?
The lighted halls long in vain
For the peal of bells that was your voice
Is the only echo emptiness?

You, life-sparkling, heiress of earth
Have you abandoned living
Tossed yourself away
To crawl into the bowels of nothingness
Bride of the self-made dark?

Sunshine girl, gone? Are you gone?
Is death-in-life your choice
Your loss, your wish?

Where are you, Karen
Or is Karen myth?

When The Heart Is Eager

Even if ears are plugged with stone
Nerves dead, no vibration in the bone
We hear, if with the heart we listen.

Even though eyes are blinded
White with cataract, red with pain
We see if we are open-minded
Still see rain-drops glisten
In the sunlight of the brain
Vividness of loss our gain
No matter if resource meager
When the heart is eager.

Ears, eyes, hands are nothing without intent
The Life-force in its longing to be well-spent
Keeps us from being impotent, absurd
Empty in gesture and in word.

The miracle of being, given us to grasp
Is ours to revel in, until the last
Sweet gasp of bursting breath...

Then, with joy exploding
Into God's universe we go
Without forboding.

Small Death, Life Large

In sleep's small death
We die
Only to be born again
Not to perish
But awaken
To each dawn
Unshaken
Another day
To claim, to cherish.

Life surges
Even as it ebbs.
Tide, sand, sun, storm
Following hidden laws
Perform
Entangling us in cosmic webs.

We on heaven's ladder climbing
Conform
To celestial timing
Respond to
Stellar pantomiming.

Listen, listen
Distant voices
Faintly, sweetly chiming...
So near, so far, so numerous
Our pinpoint lives
Made luminous
In starry light.

Constellations
In the changing skies
Reveal patterns
To unseeing eyes
Small death
Life large
Vision vast
And hope, hope
For Paradise.

You Will Not Leave Unknown

You will not go unloved
Unknown
Into anonymous night
Believer in life
In light
You will go enthroned
In inherent wisdom
Grandeur of spirit undisputed
Facing the Godhead
Without fear.

Then others
Will nod their heads sagely
Whisper loyalty
Admire your strength
Knowing all must live
On their own cross
Some unthinkable to bear.

No, you will not go
Unloved, unnamed
You will not leave unknown.

Person Unparalleled

You were there for us all
More than you knew
More than any of us knew.

We, at your memorial
Are your monument
Testament to your
On-going influence
Your incisive insight
Clarity, wit
Your peerless presence
With us yet
Unrestricted warmth
And strength
We all feel
Know and admire
Person unparalleled
Priceless in our hearts.

Too Soon For Tumbleweed

In the young years
In the cool and lonely dark
You came
Touch like fire
Kisses like hot rain.

Now in the numbing cold
In a night grown old
You toss
Sheets crackling like fallen leaves.
With each intake of your breath
In pain
The night wind grieves.

I grieve, too
A keening loss
Trembling at your hurting
Longing to hold you
Help you bear it
Whisper prayer.

Not for lack of love or spirit
Is there this long default
There is no halt
Time makes its claim
But this change
Too swiftly came.

No, no, not yet the beloved body's crumbling
Too soon, too soon for tumbleweed
Not yet the scattering
Of the soul's seed...

For this, for you
For us
For love transcendent
God, I pray
Do not take his life away.

Know Only Joy

Do not grieve
When death comes
Know only joy.
No one, no thing is lost
Change is the surge of life
Birth and death are one.
End is beginning, beginning end.
Night shades into day
Day to night
Beyond all horizons of the mind.
Intellect is not the compass
Only joy can take you there.

When death comes, rejoice!
Sing out hosannas that the tide is in
Gathering up its own to the breast of the sea.

When death comes
Bathe in its baptismal power
Its antiseptic beauty, clean of guilt.
Warm yourself deeply
In the presence of the universal
For what is man, in all his vast intelligence,
But a small sandcrab on the beach of time?

Be glad, be glad!
Sand and sea go on and on and on and on
Ever into eternity.

Is It Ever Too Late?...

Not a good night to be out. Driving was hazardous, with rain coming down in sheets.

The dark pavement seemed too dark, slippery. And such a gale! The wind whipped around, not only from the ocean, but from every direction.

At least she was wearing her black trenchcoat. There were two steps down to the quaint little cottage on Coast Highway, one of the last of its kind still in service. It had been a realtor's. Now the sign said "INSURANCE". She hesitated, then reached for the door when a sudden gust threw her against it, plunging her into the small front room.

"Pardon me," she said, laughing. "I didn't mean to burst in like that!" "My pleasure, a great pleasure," he assured her, with old-world courtliness. "In fact, I have been waiting for you."

He rose from behind the big sprawling desk. On the side was a fireplace with a roaring fire, warming and welcoming. He took her black trenchcoat, dripping wet, and hung it on the rack next to the door.

Then he seated her in the handsome upholstered chair, itself a work of art, next to him. His every move was almost ceremonial. For her it was a high moment, a new experience.

"I'm glad you came. I have been looking forward to this meeting with great expectation."

"Have you?" She was wary, somewhat skeptical, but she liked his gray hair, his demeanor, and his evident delight in seeing her.

"I have always admired you," he was saying. "You were my favorite movie star. More than Gloria Swanson, more than Greta Garbo. I followed your career. I saw every one of your films."

"You did?" How was she to respond? Being an over-the-hill celebrity was a difficult way to live a life. She was basically shy, never talkative. This time she felt even less like talking. She just liked sitting there, out of the storm, appreciated by this attractive, elegant man. He brewed tea and served it in china cups.

"You are so beautiful, with the firelight putting half your face in shadow. The kind of lighting Rembrandt liked...the great photographers..."

She did not know how to answer. But before she could think of something to say, bedlam broke loose outside. Sirens blared. Police cars, an ambulance, fire rescue vehicles materialized, lights blazing.

"Let's open the blinds wider and watch the show," he suggested.

There it was, right outside the window, the vintage Rolls Royce wrapped around the light pole. People coming from nowhere, milling around. Reporters from local newspapers, already on the job. Then, finally, seemingly interminably, the slender black-coated figure was placed on a stretcher, blanket pulled over her face. Clearly, the driver was dead. The show was over.

"Come," he invited her warmly, "let's settle in and talk." It was plain to see he was fascinated with her, doting on her and she felt pleased to be wrapped in the glow of his attention.

"So dear lady, what is the most important thing in life to you?" he asked.

She did not have to think. "Oh, love. Love, of course. I had four husbands. I loved each one of them, in different ways, I guess. I often thought, if the attributes of all four could have been in one man...it would have been...perfect!" She laughed, that still-remembered bell-like laugh that was once her trademark.

"Is it still possible to find that man?" He was looking at her with such gentleness, with such meaningfulness, she wondered, could this be the great love she had always been seeking? It was as exhilerating as a ski slope, as relaxing as a tropical beach. She was slightly uneasy that it seemed all too fast, unlikely, but somehow it was credible. This was an unbelievable evening.

After awhile, she became aware that she was losing track of place, time. She did not know how long she sat there with him, sensing his wondrous acceptance, his intuitive response. She felt dreamy, enraptured. It seemed like a long and glorious eternity, but at the same time an all too short moment. This must be what she was born for. Never had she felt so complete.

"Could you love me, my star, my dream girl?", he was asking. When she assented, he rose to embrace her and even as his arms enfolded her, she noted that her black trenchcoat was no longer there.